I Can Give

By Angie Quantrell

"I beseech you therefore, brethren, by the mercies of God, that you present your bodies a living sacrifice, holy, acceptable to God, which is your reasonable service. And do not be conformed to this world, but be transformed by the renewing of your mind, that you may prove what is that good and acceptable and perfect will of God" (Rom. 12:1–2).

I dedicate this book to my children, Taylor
and Chelsie, and my nephews, Jacob,
Zack, Joseph, Sy, Sebastian, and Cody. I
pray that you find the acceptable, good,
and perfect will of God for your lives.

Illustrated by Gayle Lopez

Woman's Missionary Union®
P.O. Box 830010
Birmingham, AL 35283-0010

Dewey Decimal Classification: CE
Subject Headings: CHILDREN'S LITERATURE

Series: I Can
ISBN: 1-56309-625-0
W038102 • 0503 • 5M

How to Use this Book

Read this book with your preschooler. Talk about the pictures and different situations that Juan Carlos and Gabriela experience. Try saying the words in Spanish.

For younger preschoolers, point out ways the brother and sister give to others.

For older preschoolers, talk about the variety of things the family does that show different ways to give. Discuss how each activity helps others.

Choose one of the suggested activities at the end of this book to do with your family. Make giving a special family habit and enjoy the time spent together helping others.

I can give thanks and praise to God.

Juan Carlos sat beside his sister, Gabriela. He looked at his family as they listened to the preacher.

"God loves us to tell Him thank You. He wants us to give Him praise," said the preacher.

Juan Carlos looked at his mamá. "Can I do that, too?" he whispered.

She smiled. "Yes," she whispered. "We can all praise God and tell Him thank You."

Juan Carlos was happy. When the music played, he sang loudly.

"I can give thanks and praise to God," Juan Carlos said to his family as they walked home.

Puedo dar gracias y alabanza a Dios.

[PWEH-doh dahr GRAH-syahs
ee ah-lah-BAHN-zah a dyohs]

I can give food.

Juan Carlos watched his mamá put several cans of corn in the cart.

"Why are we buying all of this food, Mamá?" he asked.

"Remember the family that needs food to eat?" she said.

"I remember," he said. "They don't have any food."

"Yes," replied his mother. "Jesus wants us to give to each other."

Juan Carlos smiled. He grabbed some tortillas and pinto beans. "We can give food to help them."

Puedo dar comida.
[PWEH-doh dahr coh-MEE-dah]

I can give friendship.

"Happy Birthday, Gabriela," sang Juan Carlos and his friends. Everyone was having fun.

Juan Carlos ran around the tree. A boy was standing alone there. He was crying.

Juan Carlos walked to him. "Hi," he said. "Can I be your friend?"

The boy stopped crying. He smiled at Juan Carlos. Juan Carlos led the boy to the party. *I can give by being a friend*, thought Juan Carlos.

Puedo dar la amistad.
[PWEH-doh dahr lah ah-mees-TAHD]

List for Missionaries
1. pencils
2. crayons
3. shampoo
4. toothbrush
5. toothpaste
6. combs

TOOTHBRITE

shampo

I can give supplies.

Juan Carlos and his mamá looked at a piece of paper.

"What's that?" asked Gabriela.

"It's a list," said Juan Carlos.

"It shows things that missionaries need," added Mamá.

"Oh," said Gabriela. "Are we going to send some things?"

Mamá nodded. She held up a bag. Juan Carlos put in some crayons.

"We are helping by giving supplies," said Juan Carlos.

Puedo dar útiles.
[PWEH-doh dahr OO-tee-lehs]

I can give flowers.

"Juan Carlos," called his papá. "Come and help me pick flowers."

Juan Carlos ran outside. He helped pick brightly colored flowers and put them in a vase. "What are the flowers for?" he asked.

"Mr. Garcia is sick. He's in the hospital," said Papá. "He loves flowers and visitors."

"Oh," said Juan Carlos. "We are going to help him feel better by visiting and giving him flowers."

Puedo dar flores.
[PWEH-doh dahr FLOH-rehs]

I can give my time.

Juan Carlos and Gabriela knelt on the grass. They were pulling weeds. Juan Carlos tugged hard on a stubborn weed.

"Ugh," he said as it came out and he fell backwards. He laughed. "That weed didn't want to come out."

Abuela ([ah-BWEH-lah] grandmother) smiled at Juan Carlos. "Thank you for help-ing weed my flowers. I am not able to pull weeds anymore."

Juan Carlos smiled. "I am glad that I can give my time to help you, Abuela."

Puedo dar mi tiempo.
[PWEH-doh dahr mee TYEHM-po]

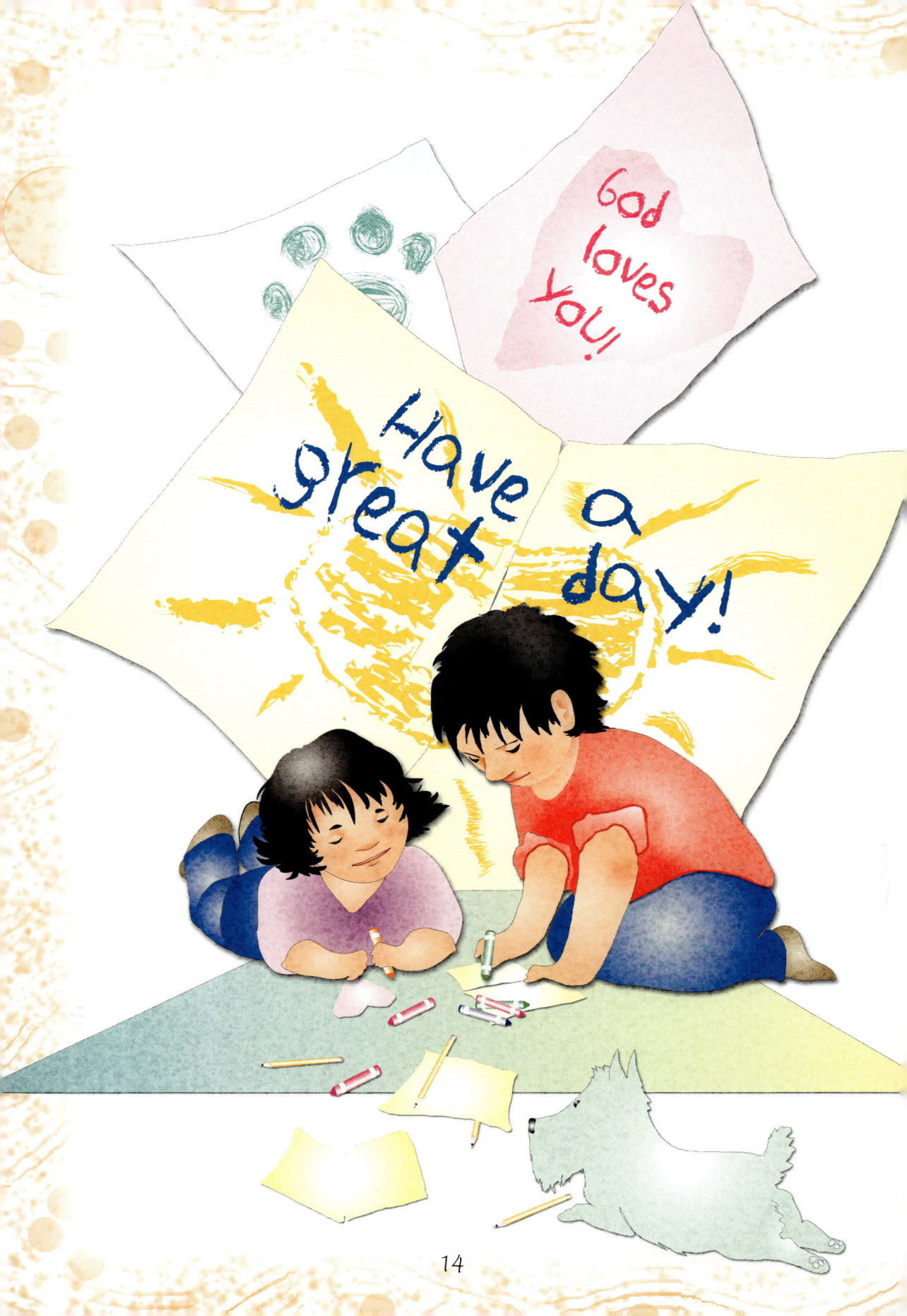

God loves you!

Have a great day!

I can give things I make.

Juan Carlos drew pictures and wrote words on pieces of paper.

"What are you doing?" asked Gabriela.

"I am making some cards," said Juan Carlos.

"Why?" asked Gabriela.

"My teacher told me about some people who can't get to church," said Juan Carlos. "She said they were lonely, and would like to get mail from us."

"Oh," said Gabriela, "you mean shut-ins. Can I make cards, too?"

"Sure," said Juan Carlos. "We can give things we make."

Puedo dar las cosas que hago.
[PWEH-doh dahr lahs COH-sahs keh AH-go]

I can give my help.

"Jack," called Juan Carlos.

"Rruff, rruff," barked Jack as he raced to his clean water dish.

Juan Carlos watched his dog lap up water with his pink tongue. Jack wagged his tail as he looked at Juan Carlos. "You know what's next, don't you, Jack?" asked Juan Carlos.

Juan Carlos poured crunchy dog food into Jack's food dish. "Here you go," said Juan Carlos.

Mamá walked into the room. "Thanks for doing your chores," she said.

Juan Carlos watched Jack gobble his dinner. "I can give my help."

Puedo dar mi ayuda.
[PWEH-doh dahr mee ah-YOO-dah]

17

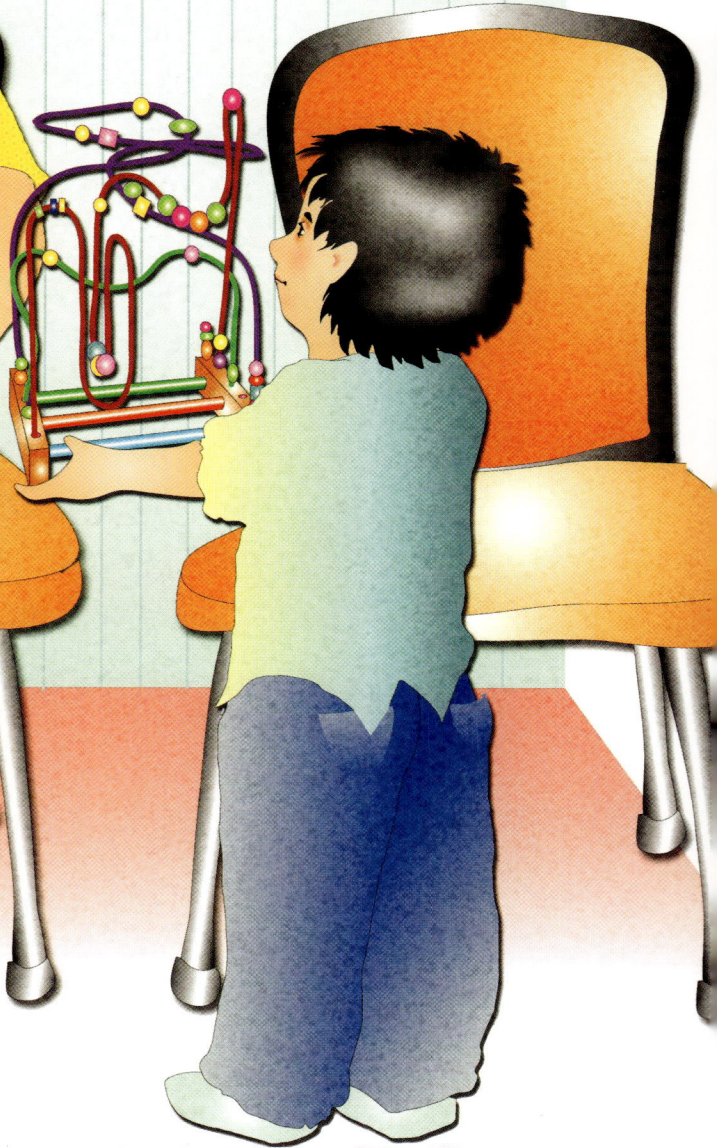

18

I can give my things.

Juan Carlos played with the maze. He was waiting with his mamá to see the doctor.

"Wah-wah," cried a small child.

Juan Carlos looked at the little girl. What should he do?

Suddenly, he smiled. He knew how to help. Juan Carlos carried the maze to the girl. "Would you like to play with this?" asked Juan Carlos.

The little girl stopped crying. Juan Carlos showed her how to play with the maze. *I can give my things and make others feel better,* thought Juan Carlos.

Puedo dar mis cosas.
[PWEH-doh dahr mees COH-sahs]

I can give my energy.

"Here we go," said Juan Carlos and Gabriela's papá. "Time to help serve the food."

Gabriela put on plastic gloves to serve milk.

"What am I going to do?" asked Juan Carlos.

"Here," said Mamá. "Give each person a corn muffin."

Juan Carlos put on plastic gloves and placed muffins on many different plates.

Juan Carlos grinned at Mamá. "I can give my energy to help others," said Juan Carlos.

Puedo dar mi energía.
[PWEH-doh dahr mee eh-nehr-HEE-ah]

I can give love.

Juan Carlos kicked the soccer ball down the field. He ran after it.

"Look out," yelled Papá, who was watching the game.

Juan Carlos saw his friend trip over the ball and fall down hard.

"Marisa," said Juan Carlos as he ran to her, "are you OK?"

Marisa was crying. She had a huge scrape on her elbow. Juan Carlos carefully gave Marisa a big hug.

Marisa stopped crying. "Thanks, Juan Carlos. I always feel better after a hug."

I can give love to others, thought Juan Carlos.

Puedo dar el amor.
[PWEH-doh dahr ehl ah-MOHR]

I can give the love of Jesus.

Juan Carlos helped his papá load a box of Bibles into the car. "We have many Bibles," said Papá.

"Bibles," said Juan Carlos, "tell us all about Jesus. What are you doing with them?"

"I am going to give them to homeless people," said Papá.

"Can I help give the Bibles?" said Juan Carlos.

"I was counting on your help," said Papá as he buckled his seatbelt.

"When I give a Bible to someone, it can help them learn about Jesus. I can give them Jesus," said Juan Carlos as he got in the car.

Puedo dar el amor de Jesús a los demás.

[PWEH-doh dahr ehl ah-MOHR deh heh-SOOS ah lohs deh-MAHS]

I can give.

Juan Carlos poured his money into the jar. "It's finally full," he shouted to Gabriela.

"Now we can take our offering to church," said Gabriela.

The next Sunday, Juan Carlos and Gabriela emptied their jar into the big offering plate. They felt good to give their money to help others.

Juan Carlos smiled as he thought about all of the ways he was learning to give.

Juan Carlos tugged on Mamá's sleeve. She looked at him.

"I can give," said Juan Carlos.

Puedo dar.
[PWEH-doh dahr]

A Note to Parents

Giving is a habit of a healthy Christian lifestyle. Generosity is one of the fruits of a growing relationship with our heavenly Father. God calls on us, His children, to have giving spirits, cheerful attitudes, and helping hands. He commands us to love each other, cheerfully give, and be His hands in this world.

When God talks about giving, He is not speaking only of money. He wants us to give generously of our time, our energy, our talents, our hearts, our resources, and our blessings. God is the giver of all we possess. He speaks to us in our heart's ear, guiding us in ways to give and share the many blessings that come from Him.

Our Father tells us to train our children in His ways. He wants us to teach our preschoolers and family members about giving and helping others. As a parent, your most important responsibility is to show your preschooler how to love and give. Demonstrate a giving attitude and loving heart to your family. They will learn by your example.

Use your creativity to find ways to give. With your preschooler and family members, make a list of giving activities. Vote for the favorite ideas. Plan to do one family giving activity a month. Make a scrapbook of giving activities. Look back upon the fun your family has had participating in giving activities.

Our Father, who will see your generous spirit and actions, will pour down blessings upon you and your family.

Bible Thoughts to Use with Preschoolers

Bring an offering (see 1 Chron. 16:29).

It is a good thing to give thanks to God (see Psalm 92:1).

Jesus went about doing good (see Acts 10:38).

God loves a cheerful giver (see 2 Cor. 9:7).

Help one another (see Gal. 5:13).

The Bible is useful for teaching us how to live (see 2 Tim. 3:16).

Read More About It (For Parents)

To learn more about giving, read the following verses in the Bible. Memorize these verses and use them in your everyday activities.

Leviticus 27:30

Deuteronomy 15:10–11

Malachi 3:10

Matthew 6:19–21

John 3:16

1 Corinthians 3:9

1 Corinthians 10:31

1 Timothy 6:17–19

Hebrews 13:15–16

Giving Activities

Field Trip for Fido. Arrange for your family to visit a local nursing home, and include your pet dog, cat, or other small animal. As you travel to the nursing home, talk about the giving of time and attention you will be sharing with residents, as well as what family members should expect during the visit. At the home, visit with residents, allowing time for petting, holding, and hugging pets. Take pictures and make copies to give to residents. Make plans to visit regularly with your pet and your family.
Caution: Watch pets at all times. Supervise carefully.

Clipping Coupons. Materials: advertising that includes coupons, scissors, notepad

Enlist your family to help you look for and cut out cents off coupons for items you purchase. Watch for food, household, or restaurant coupons. As you shop, allow preschoolers to give coupons to clerks when you pay for services or items. Keep track in the notebook of the amount of money the coupons save you. Total the coupon savings, and give the same amount to a missions offering. Tell preschoolers what missions project or offering the money will be used for.

Clothing and Toy Donation. Decorate a large cardboard box with pictures and a sign reading _My Give-Away Box._ During the cleaning of closets, dressers, and toy boxes, help your preschooler choose outgrown clothes and toys. Place them in the decorated box. Together, donate them to your church's clothing closet or women's shelter. Talk about how giving donated items can help others.

Cleanup, Cleanup, Everybody Cleanup. Organize a neighborhood cleanup day. Have family members create and distribute flyers to neighbors informing them of the day and time for cleanup day. Ask neighbors to bring garbage sacks and gloves. As you work together to pick up trash, place recyclable items in a separate container. Talk about being a good steward and giving time to take care God's creation. Invite neighbors to enjoy cookies and punch in your yard when the cleanup is complete.
Tip: Cash in recyclables, and give money to a missions offering.